Katie the Ladybug
Explaining Emotions of Grief to a Child

By: **Jesse E. Roberts**

Illustrations: **Rachel Adams**

D0920664

Dedicated to the loving memory of my Mother and Father, and to the glory of my Lord and Savior Jesus Christ – Without whom I would be nothing.

Katie the Ladybug: Explaining Emotions of Grief to a Child

ISBN: 978-0-9827003-9-6

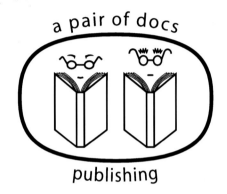

a pair of docs publishing
www.apairofdocspublishing.com
P.O. Box 972, Boiling Springs, North Carolina 28017-0972
704-473-0346

Printed by **BP Solutions Group, Inc.**
Asheville, NC

"Jesse Roberts has written a thoughtful, developmentally sound book for grieving youngsters. Adults will find it to be a valuable resource for helping children understand the nature and feelings of loss."

Jackson Rainer, Ph.D., ABPP
Psychologist and researcher on grief and bereavement.

"Jesse Roberts' *Katie the Ladybug: Explaining Emotions of Grief to a Child* is a wonderful addition to children's literature on grief and loss. In this sensitive and beautifully illustrated book, Roberts offers a simple yet critical message – we grieve in many ways as the unique individuals that we are. Both children and adults can benefit from the powerful validation of that message."

Kenneth J. Doka, Ph.D.
Professor, The College of New Rochelle
Senior consultant, The Hospice Foundation of America
Author, Living with Grief: Children and Adolescents

Rachel Adams, illustrator of the artwork in this book, wrote and illustrated her first book when she was only six-years-old. It was a retelling of a high-school age adventure of mine – a children's book. Now as a young adult, Rachel continues to polish her skills for her passion for art and literature. The artwork and illustrations in this children's book are her contribution for both wounded children and the adults who love them. Rachel is now working on a Master's degree in English Literature and her license to become a Yoga Instructor. Her goal is to achieve a doctorate in Irish Literature.

Her father, **Bob Adams**

Katie the Ladybug was one in a family of eight.

She and her brothers and sisters lived in the garden with their Mommy and Daddy.

There was Molly, Polly,
Mindy, Cindy, Jack,
Bobby and Bruce.

Katie and her siblings played in the garden together all the time.

One day Katie
became very sick.

She could no longer play with her brothers and sisters. Instead, all she could do was lie in her favorite tulip.

One day Katie's parents called a family meeting. Everyone knew something was wrong as soon as they heard the tone of their Mommy's voice.

"Katie is no longer with us," Mommy said with a tear in her eye. "She has become a part of the garden."

This news made Molly very sad.

It seemed like all she could do was cry because she missed Katie so badly.

Polly was very angry.

She did not understand why Katie had to leave so soon. It didn't seem fair.

Mindy became jealous.

She was the youngest of her siblings, and no one was paying her any attention. She felt deserted and alone.

Cindy became very anxious.

Everyone around her was upset, and she didn't know how to feel. All she knew was that life was different without Katie.

Jack became very fearful when Katie died.

He was afraid something would happen to him, or to his other brothers and sisters, and he wasn't ready to lose anyone else.

Bobby felt very guilty when Katie passed away.

He had gotten in an argument with her just before she became sick, and did not have the chance to apologize to her. He wished things would have been different.

Bruce missed Katie a lot, but he was very happy that she was not sick anymore.

He knew she was better off as a part of the garden – without pain and suffering.

Katie's parents loved her very much, and missed her terribly. They experienced all kinds of emotions when she died. Some days they were sad, and other days they were angry. Some days were easier for them than others.

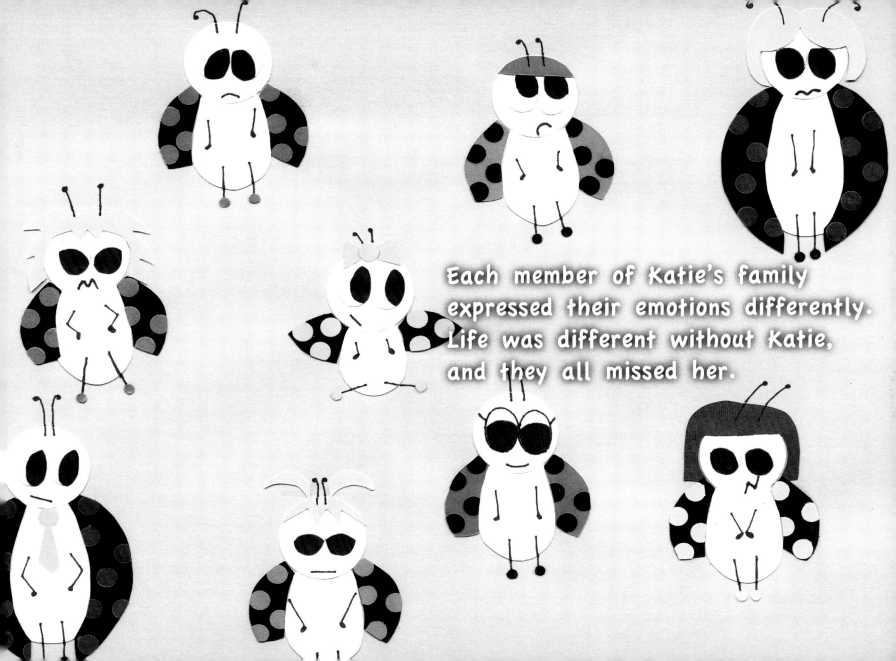

Each member of Katie's family expressed their emotions differently. Life was different without Katie, and they all missed her.

All they could do was remember the good times they had with her and find comfort in the fact that they would one day see her again, when they too became a part of the garden.

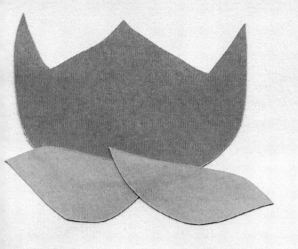

The End

Questions for Discussion

- Which character is the most like you?

- How do you feel when you think of losing someone you love?

- What are some healthy ways for us to deal with our emotions?

- What are healthy ways that you can remember your loved ones?